DWANE FRITZ GERALD

Crank It Up!

Harnessing The Synergies of Team Belief

I dedicate this book to the "Crank It Up Gang" of 2013 and beyond. Everyone who took part in that movement. We created history together. May you continue to defy the odds and have fun while doing so.
Team Crank It Up for Life!

Contents

1

The Vision

It has been six months since Aubyn stepped into the role of interim operations manager. Last month, the productivity slide bottomed out at a dismal 22.4 moves per crane hour (MPCH).

"Under normal circumstances, we should achieve upwards of 25 moves per crane hour, or thereabouts; that's what the terminal was designed to achieve," mused Aubyn.

These circumstances were anything but normal. The metrics that showed the maintenance department's performance against the key performance indicators (KPIs) were the worst on record. The management and staff there felt utterly demoralized. They felt they needed to get the much-needed support from The Authority.

The maintenance department team had to mothball upwards of 20% and, in specific instances, as much as 30% of the various container handling equipment. They had even been cannibalizing the mothballed equipment to secure spare parts to keep the active fleet going.

In the main, the terminal's tarmac had fallen into disrepair, further exacerbating the strain on the availability and reliability of mobile equipment. STS crane operators complained regularly about the state of the crane rails. The cries from the maintenance and operations department grew louder with each passing day.

All categories of equipment operators lost confidence in operating the equipment to its optimally designed capacity, resulting in a slowdown in productivity.

The performance metrics on ship-to-shore (STS crane) reliability, straddle carrier availability, and crane productivity were embarrassing, and shipping companies were using these poor metrics to threaten legal and other drastic consequences.

Such was the condition of the terminal. Despite the difficulties of the last six months, Aubyn had been proactive, advocating a "back to basics" philosophy. He successfully implemented or reinforced most things he would have wanted. He enforced rigorous compliance with the Terminal Operating System (TOS), harnessing innovative technology to oversee it around the clock.

The operation teams seldom accurately reported poor performances. It was common for actual performance figures to be doctored, leading to false reporting.

To verify the productivity reports from each Shift Manager, Aubyn depended on his Revenue Protection Team, especially Clayton and Denton, who had become experts at sifting out anomalies.

Aubyn didn't shy away from pushing his managers for truthful reporting.

"The KPIs may be grim, but at least they're accurate, showing us the true state of affairs. We can't fix what we won't acknowledge. Once we recognize the problem, we can tackle it. If we can identify the issue, we can find a solution," he said.

One thing that gave him some solace was the improved overall atmosphere among the staff. There was more friendly banter, and a sense of lightheartedness had taken over. Even the weekly management meetings Aubyn had just emerged from had become more relaxed.

Notwithstanding the improvement in the social environment, Aubyn knew it would require more to rally his team and the entire workforce. The terminal was going to the dogs, and everyone knew it, evidenced by a lack of significant capital investment, poor performance metrics, and low staff morale.

The talks of the impending privatization seem to grow louder every day. Whenever the news mentioned the port, it focused on the government's plans to privatize the assets that had become a burden the taxpayers could no longer afford.

Here comes David puffing on a cigarette as usual, with his trademark childish smirk, ever the prankster. He is up to no good; some unsuspecting soul is about to be on the wrong end of his wit. This morning, it was the turn of his friend Aubyn, recently one of his most frequent victims. Truth be told, they both enjoy taking turns at each other.

David was waving a makeshift sign that read "28" in jest. He was flashing that "28" like a blinking neon sign: "28", now you see it, now you don't, hinting at the pivotal operational KPI of 28 MPCH.

"Are you still a movie star?" he asked. "Are you still acting as Ops Manager? Captain B will not confirm you, Aubyn, unless we hit 28!"

Now, 28 was a significant number on the port. Twenty-eight moves per crane hour is a weighted monthly average. It has been the single most critical productivity KPI for the last four years, the attainment of which would almost certainly result in a hefty incentive payment midway through the following month.

The incentive scheme comprised three metrics: productivity

of 28 MPCH or greater, crane reliability of 98.1% or greater, and straddle carrier availability of 89% or greater. Productivity had a weight of 60%, crane reliability 25%, and straddle carrier availability a weight of 15%.

Four years ago, the terminal's management adjusted it from 26 MPCH to 28 MPCH, and its contribution to the computation of incentive payout increased in importance to its current weighting of 60%. Conversely, other KPIs deemed less significant had their importance reduced and taken out of the computation for incentive payment. Employees consistently achieved these now lesser-weighted metrics before the adjustments, which resulted in incentive payouts.

The workforce deemed these changes as just another sleight of hand by management, setting an unattainable target to cheat the "little man" out of his fair share of the pie. All talk of incentives by management and staff alike consequently died a natural death.

However, the KPIs remained significant to the management team and the port's customers, especially the shipping lines patronizing the facilities. The achievement of these KPIs reduced variable costs associated with vessel operations and increased overall customer satisfaction.

In the container terminal industry, where productivity is king, you are only as good as your last performance. That's the nature of the container terminal industry, especially an 80% transshipment terminal; international customers have you by the proverbial nuts.

Back to the diabolical David, flashing his hypnotic sign "28". He and Aubyn had been a part of several attempts in the past to analyze and implement initiatives to raise the port's profile. They both believe much more could be done to improve the port's current state, not least to help the terminal achieve consistency in its performance toward eventually attaining some of these elusive KPIs.

Aubyn took David's teasing in stride, recognizing a kernel of truth in the playful challenge.

"Actually, you're onto something," Aubyn replied, much to David's surprise.

That was not the reaction David hoped he would have gotten. The look in Aubyn's eyes was familiar to David—it told David that he had just bitten off more than he could chew and that this attempt at banter would come back to haunt him. That look meant they were about to venture out on one of their missions to change the world, if not perhaps significantly boost the terminal's performance. At a minimum, they felt a sense of purpose for a couple of weeks before their efforts were frustrated because of a lack of buy-in.

David ruefully thought, "Why did I stir up Aubyn today?"

He knew this playful jab could lead to more work on his plate.

Yet, this moment was unique. It held potential, though only the acting operations manager, Aubyn, had the authority to lead change.

Aubyn was the unexpected choice of Captain B to head up the operations department, which came on the heels of yet another of their missions to bring change and hope. They set out seven months before to analyze the use of the ever-dwindling resources in the operations department. They intended to chart the path towards improving resource efficiency—David focusing on safety and procedures, Aubyn optimizing the TOS usage, and reducing unproductive delays.

"David doesn't realize that he is on to something. There is no reason we can't achieve the 28 moves per crane or any other KPI.

We have top-notch equipment operators and a workforce that is second to none. All we need to do as a team is dream it, believe it, and consistently motivate each other towards achieving our goals," Aubyn thought.

David inadvertently was holding up his makeshift sign not 20 feet away from the KPI Notice Board, which was last updated over a year ago.

This sparked an idea in Aubyn.

"Yes, that's it! Communicate the goal and make it visible to all," Aubyn exclaimed.

"Revive the KPI notice board, update it daily, and let every person who walks through the terminal gates see how we are doing against our monthly targets," Aubyn concluded.

Key Personal Introspection #1

Have a clear vision:
·*OWN: Become one with the vision*
·*FEEL: Desire the outcome of the vision*
·*DO: Take action towards achieving the goals*
·*LOVE: Be passionate about achieving the goals*
·*DECLARE: Verbalize the vision by sharing it with others*
·*SEE: Visualize the outcome, see beyond the surface*
·*CLARIFY: Meticulously document the various components of the vision for public consumption*

2

Owning The Vision

"Lord, have mercy! Del! Aubyn is heading towards the Radio Room. I hope he's coming to bother you and not me," Mel exclaimed.

"Quick! Ensure all the batteries are on the charger and everything's in order. Stay on your toes; you know how he can go on and on if he spots something amiss," Del exclaimed.

"Hail! Wat a gwan?" That was Aubyn's usual way of greeting a group before he individually acknowledged the ladies or engaged in banter with the gents. Some people could expect "special" treatment, especially if they were skilled at exchanging banter; a brief but lively sparring session was on the horizon.

But after his initial greetings this morning, he immediately delved into questions about the KPI Notice Board. That was unusual; he didn't pick on Del or Mel. Would there be no banter this morning?

Those who knew him well recognized this mood. He had the bit between his teeth. He had an idea for a new tweak. Over the past six months, there have been several of these tweaks. They looked forward to them because many improvements came from their suggestions.

Aubyn ensured he gave credit to the originators of these suggestions and encouraged all team members to take ownership of the resultant change process. Once the change was beneficial, he would complement the team for its efforts and the impact on the big picture.

The big picture was one of Aubyn's favorite topics, the essence of which was his core beliefs and operational philosophy.

"Why aren't we updating the KPI notice board? Do we have everything required to update it? What's our current monthly crane productivity? Do we know how to generate the KPI reports? Let me show you how to access the data." Aubyn fired away.

Before the ladies could respond, he conducted an impromptu training session at a workstation. Everyone was attentive, and by the end of the lesson, they knew how to generate KPI results and understood the importance of daily updates.

"No problem, Boss. That's our responsibility, and we'll take care of it. We didn't think it mattered because it seemed no one was paying attention," Del assured him.

With the KPI matter out of the way, Aubyn lightened the mood with a few preemptive blows, so began five minutes of jesting. The tables quickly turned; now, Aubyn was at their mercy. He made for the exit as briskly as he had entered thirty minutes ago, knowing that it would be payback time for someone when he returned to check on their progress the next day. Those in the Radio Room would feel his wrath. They won that banter session, but he would be more lyrically agile tomorrow.

"That's it! We're going for the record. If not this month, we'll achieve 28 moves per hour within the next three months."

Aubyn was resolute in his thought. His heart raced with

excitement as his adrenaline kicked into overdrive. Positive thinking inspired a vision and gave life to a dream. Just then, something was birth within him, leading the terminal and himself in a direction beyond what he could have foreseen.

"We can achieve anything if we believe and set our minds to it. We're the best, even if we have yet to realize it. This terminal is a sleeping giant waiting to be awakened." Aubyn continued.

The next step was to share this vision with the planning and execution teams. But Aubyn most relished the one-on-one interactions he would have with as many people as he would encounter, both within and outside the company.

These interactions were a source of inspiration and motivation for getting up and going to work every morning. Being on the port was more than a job for Aubyn; it was his passion and purpose.

Key Personal Introspection # 2

Take ownership of your vision by believing:
   ·Fuel the vision with positive thoughts and action
   ·Your vision should be potent. Able to awaken your desires and provoke powerful emotions
   ·Communicate your vision frequently and seek the buy-in of team members
   ·Team members who have bought into your vision will embrace it as their own
   ·Be willing to share ownership of what has become a shared vision

3

Building Relationships

It was not always like this with Aubyn. He was a natural introvert who preferred to watch life unfold from the safety of his retreat. He found solace in its tranquil haven. His favorite pastime was observing people as they navigated their daily lives.

As this armchair psychologist observed, his mind buzzed with questions, each more intriguing than the last. Conjuring up and ruminating on the ensuing thoughts. What were they thinking as they went about their business? How were they feeling, hidden behind the masks we all wear? Aubyn often wondered if he could influence their moods, perhaps even inspire them.

On a deeper level, he contemplated whether these individuals shared the same fears, insecurities, dreams, and aspirations as he did. He yearned for the day when he could bridge the gap between his introspective world and the lives of those around him, hoping that a shared connection might enrich, as mutual understanding could bring about a profound change. If only they could commune on common ground.

To the best of his knowledge, Aubyn developed this deep sense of insecurity while attending one of the most prestigious high schools on the island. Aubyn never felt he belonged, as most students were from a different socioeconomic upbringing; most of his cohorts were from the ruling class and elite circles. Although his all-round sporting prowess brought him much admiration and notice, he remained self-conscious of his working-class background.

A rethink of his aloof and reclusive mindset began over twenty years ago when the then eighteen-year-old, right out of high school, landed a job at the port as a Gate Pass Clerk in one of the freight warehouses.

For the first time in recent memory, he felt at home in his new environment, where he thought he mattered and desired to make an impact.

Aubyn had only recently started working on the port when he had a fateful interaction with Sis Pat from his church. She had come to the port to clear some personal effects shipped to her.

She recognized and warmly greeted him. But he didn't recognize her then and had no clue who she was. Somewhat embarrassed and penitent from the encounter, he took Sis Pat's loving admonishment to heart, and her gentle reproach made him reconsider his aloofness.

She told him, "Bro Aubyn, you'd know me if you mingled more. You underestimate the impact you can have. We care and want to really know you. Don't just observe—engage, even with just a greeting or chitchat. It means more than you think, and you never know how you might be called to serve."

Her words were hard to hear but resonated deeply, leaving him feeling valued. Sis Pat had a way with words; even if it was bitter medicine, it was sweet to the soul, and you left her presence feeling loved and valued.

Some ten years later, another incident challenged his perceptions further. As an office lad, he fell prey to the white-collar viewpoint that the typical blue-collar worker did not grasp the business's fundamentals. And that they were inherently lazy and were only concerned with milking the company for as much salary and benefits as they could grab.

It is easy to fall into that trap of management vs. staff or the "big man" vs. the "small man." Frankly, both sides must bear their fair share of guilt. However, the heavier burden falls on the management team, the big man. They are typically privileged with a higher education and positioned to be change agents.

Aubyn would soon learn that this myth about who was more educated formally or otherwise was just that: a fable. He discovered the treasure trove of wisdom and enlightened reasoning emanating from the shop floor, forged by a collective experience of overcoming obstacles and significant life challenges. Also, many of the younger staff members were highly qualified.

By this point, Aubyn was a Terminal Operating System (TOS) superuser working out of the information technology department. He had transitioned from operations, where he was a vessel planner.

The newly hired Training Manager, David, is waiting to be buzzed in at the office door. Aubyn, seated closest to the door, did the honors.

"Aubyn, I have a job for you. I want you to come and rap with a batch of equipment operators completing their safety training today. You can share with them how the TOS works and answer questions they might have about some issues they face as end-users," said David.

"While I could ask someone from Operations, I would rather they not conduct this session. The operators think that someone from a different department should address their concerns because they believe the TOS is not being effectively used. Word has it you were the Systems Guru," David insisted.

Instantaneously, David's request triggered Aubyn's internal dialogue of fear and self-doubt. It defaulted him into an introverted mindset and a sense of impending doom. Maybe Sis Pat's voice, which he heard replaying in his subconscious, jolted him back to the present moment.

"Now, what on earth do you want me to talk to a bunch of operators about David? These guys don't even know me. Vasil knows the TOS just as well as I do. We both went from operations to IT together as superusers. Now he is back in operations and responsible for the very thing you want me to talk about; he could do it."

David must have sensed the insecurity in Aubyn's voice, or maybe it was the pale look on his face. All the color had drained away, leaving him looking pale and frightened, as if he had just seen a ghost.

"They are waiting for you; just rap with them about how the TOS works. You may not know the operators, but they have heard about you, the System's Guru, who fixes all their problems whenever the TOS is acting up."

"By the way, even if you tell them a load of crap about the backend of the system, they won't even realize that you are talking crap; plus, I will be there to control and moderate the conversation," David reassured him.

"So come, let's go!" David motioned.

Despite initial reluctance and a flood of self-doubt, he remembered Sis Pat's words and agreed.

That day was the first time David and Aubyn teamed up, the first of many projects to come. On that fateful day, many bonds were forged, and many preconceptions and misconceptions died during that hour-long rap session.

Neither David nor Aubyn could have predicted the implications of this one hour. Notwithstanding, it laid a pathway that had far-reaching implications in the not-too-distant future.

Over the next few weeks, he led at least three more such sessions with successive groups of operators. Each was as meaningful as the first- at least to Aubyn, who always remembered those sessions fondly. That session, and the subsequent ones, broke down barriers and changed perspectives.

Aubyn and David formed a strong partnership, and Aubyn discovered the operators' deep understanding and commitment to the company. He realized those on the ground had invaluable insights and practical ideas that could significantly enhance the company's operations.

Aubyn now realized how much the average worker cared about fixing the systemic issues plaguing the entity and how much they had gleaned about the company's direction from being on the frontline.

In addition, he gained invaluable insight into how the life of a typical worker and their families were deeply connected to the company's success. Like him, they shared a vested interest in the company's wellbeing.

Key Personal Introspection # 3

Build meaningful relationships:
 ·Be willing to come out of your comfort zone
 ·Be less self-centered
 ·Focus on meeting the needs of others

·*Listen*
·*Communicate with love and humility*
·*Demonstrate compassion and empathy*
·*Be available to be used*

4

Seizing The Moment

The universe seems to conspire with a man on a mission. Aubyn's baptism into senior operations management taught him to recognize when this phenomenon was happening - when the stars were in alignment. As a result, he had become more adept at seizing the moment.

Aubyn had just barely escaped the Radio Room onslaught, with his dignity hanging on by the thinnest of threads, when he caught sight of Adrian, "The Chief" (chief union delegate), making his way from the punch-clock.

"Chief! What's up, bro? Do you have a minute?" Aubyn inquired.

They were never what you would term bosom buddies, but they shared a mutual respect for each other, not least of which they were both men of faith.

"Chief, what has become of the PIS, the Productivity Incentive Scheme? Is it still applicable? I mean, is it still binding? What if the staff should achieve the KPIs that trigger an incentive payout? What do you expect would happen?" Aubyn fired away.

Aubyn's rapid-fire questions about the PIS and the potential

16

for incentive payouts showed that he still had the bit firmly gripped between his molars.

The Chief knew Aubyn already knew the answers to his rhetorical questions. It was clear from Aubyn's tone that he was seeking The Chief's help, not an uncommon occurrence. But the Chief clearly received the message. It was not the first time the acting operations manager had reached out to the union, nor would it be the last.

"Well, Aubyn, the incentive scheme is still binding. Not everybody is happy about that fact. You know how they adjusted it the last time to make it more difficult for the worker to achieve. They made all attempts to put it out of the reach of the staff." The Chief began cautiously.

"But I will get you a signed copy of the agreement so you can peruse it yourself. The union is always ready to support anything that benefits the workers and the port. I am not optimistic about your other team members' support, but the workers will support all well-meaning efforts."

"Personally, though, I won't make any promises to the workforce that I cannot guarantee. I have seen them get all worked up before, only to be disappointed because of unfulfilled commitments." The Chief continued matter-of-factly.

"So, you know what you need to do with your management team; we, the workers and the union, will do our part," the Chief concluded.

He gave a balanced and honest answer, one coming from the very depth of his heart.

With that said, the Chief took a firm grip of Aubyn's hand and looked him dead in the eyes as they shook hands. Both men understood each other, that which was spoken and that which could not be uttered. After this exchange, they parted ways, the hidden messages echoing as loudly as the spoken ones.

"The message was clear from the Chief," Aubyn recapped. I need to talk to the man who controls the purse strings. Arnoldo.

After being acknowledged, Aubyn entered the CFO's office.

"Arnoldo, how are you doing? Tell me something: Is the PIS still in play? If the guys hit the target this month, will there be the expected payout?" Aubyn interrogated.

Arnoldo was cunning and savvy enough to tread carefully with his response. The answer he gave was consequently a politically correct one.

"Yes, Aubyn, the PIS is still binding, and the management will comply with the terms set out therein. We are obliged to do so. Does that mean your team will make a run at it? Do you really think the target is attainable, given the issues in the maintenance department?" Arnoldo responded.

Sometimes, others' doubts can fuel your resolve to prove them wrong. So Arnoldo's expressions of doubt were all that Aubyn needed to further stoke the fire of his determination burning deep within him.

Aubyn responded quickly and confidently,

"The guys will be fired up and ready to rumble. Ensure the company is prepared to pay the incentive in the next few months."

Arnoldo was no ordinary finance man; he wheeled significant influence over the staff and had his fingers on the organization's pulse. He was not only the heir apparent to Captain B but also the trusted confidant of Nigel, aka "The Man," who was the head of the authority. Nothing of real significance took place on the port without the sanctioning of The Man.

Arnoldo recognized that behind the cocky candor of Aubyn, somewhere in there, there was a cry for help. Arnoldo had to ponder how and if he wanted to lend a helping hand to his brash junior colleague.

Ultimately, Arnoldo knew that supporting Aubyn's efforts could benefit the organization. A lift in productivity would release some of the mounting pressures he faced. Because of the underwhelming below-par terminal performance, the hard-wheeling shipping companies had stepped up their pressure campaign.

"If they were to achieve anywhere close to the 28 moves per hour, this would give me considerable breathing room. I am facing constant threats from the shipping lines and mounting claims that I have to be honoring month after month. I will definitely encourage Aubyn's efforts." Arnoldo thought to himself with a sense of foreboding mixed with expectancy.

"A productivity of 26 moves per hour approaching 28 moves per hour would be perfect," Arnoldo thought.

"That would go far in convincing The Authority to pay a gratuity around Christmas to offset the perennial contentious bonus discussion come year's end. Happier customers and happier staff, that sounds like a win-win." Concluded Arnoldo.

"Mission accomplished," Aubyn thought.

"I heard what I needed to hear precisely. Both the company and the union still recognized the validity of the current Productivity Incentive Scheme. The rest is politics, and that is above my pay grade. Let Arnoldo deal with that; my job was to meet targets."

Aubyn knew that timing was critical; there was a window of opportunity that must be exploited quickly. Aubyn had been around the port long enough to know nothing stays static, especially in a challenging economic environment. And he knew external constraints influenced the port's management.

Therefore, it was easy for the port's management to renegotiate any existing agreement.

The Chief would have been aware of this reality and had intimated the same in his brief conversation with Aubyn moments earlier. Even the hesitancy in Arnoldo's voice and politically correct answer had also borne that out.

Key Personal Introspection # 4

Seize the moment, live in the NOW:
   ·In every crisis, there is an opportunity waiting
   ·Be prepared
   ·Be proactive
   ·Act NOW, don't procrastinate
   ·Be receptive to others
   ·Ask for help in humility
   ·Receive help with gratitude

5

Build a Core Team

As the adage goes, the devil is in the details. This moment demanded absolute clarity; Aubyn needed to seek wisdom from his mentor. Nathan, the cerebral architect of the PIS computation, known as "The Professor," would be his source.

Some thirteen years prior, Nathan had taken Aubyn under his tutelage. Nathan saw potential in Aubyn's knack for technology and his relentless drive as a vessel planner in the operations department.

During another phase of the company's reshuffling exercise, Nathan recommended Aubyn as one of two key players to bridge the divide between the operations and IT departments.

Those were exciting times for the company as it transitioned from a primarily manual operation to one driven by the then-embryonic tech-centric approach.

A year before the terminal implemented a new Terminal Operating System, Aubyn received a promotion to Vessel Planner. He played a pivotal role in the system's implementation and adoption. A role tailor-made for him because of his youthful tech-savvy and the fact that Aubyn was currently studying as a part-time college student majoring in Information Technology.

As the IT department's lead, Nathan was the nucleus of technological innovations at the port and held the trust of the top brass. For innovative or technical insight and operational strategy, Nigel often sought Nathan's counsel. Aubyn would spend six years working under the tutelage of Nathan in the IT department as a superuser before his return to operations.

Two years before Aubyn's promotion to acting operations manager, Nathan would come to his rescue. By then, Aubyn was one of three senior operations managers. However, his operational philosophy conflicted with those of his peers. Hence, something had to give, prompting a need for change.

Nathan was happy to harness Aubyn's tenacity and assertiveness, so he appointed him the process implementation manager in the newly established business solutions department. Just the lifeline Aubyn needed to resuscitate his floundering career. However, Aubyn and Nathan's paths diverged once more.

The Authority recalled Captain B from retirement to steer the terminal through another crisis. Captain B was Nigel's go-to guy to stabilize the ship in times of storm, as it was not the first time Nigel had taken him out of retirement to pilot the terminal through choppy seas. Nathan was reassigned to The Authority, and Samuel took over the business solutions department.

"I must consult The Professor," Aubyn mused. He dialed Nathan's number.

"Prof, I need your guidance. We aim to attain the crane productivity KPI and trigger the incentive payment. I need your help to understand the computations' details," Aubyn inquired.

"The details are being sent to you immediately. I'm also developing a real-time KPI Dashboard that could be useful to you. It tracks the performance of several key indicators in the operations. You will have a copy of the trial version by the end of today. Feel free to test it out and provide me with feedback, and if there are any other metrics you are interested in having displayed, please let me know," said Nathan.

"It seems the Maintenance metrics are posing some real challenges for operations, so this tool should assist both teams in managing their performance," Nathan responded, always one step ahead with his technological foresight.

This was Nathan at his core; he was a proactive innovator who often provided solutions before they were sought. But to Aubyn, Nathan was that and more. Nathan was always supportive of him and an eager kingmaker who helped to steer his career trajectory.

Aubyn knew he could count on Nathan to have his back. Nathan's innovativeness and understanding of the operations would prove invaluable to this mission.

"All well with everyone?" You-all good? Aubyn greeted the planning office staff, offering personalized salutations to the ladies first. He then casually inquired about the productivity rate, a figure he was already privy to.

The staff knew he knew the numbers, yet they expected his queries as a test of their knowledge. Knowing was their business, and they have become accustomed to knowing. Some of them, out of a genuine interest, while others just wanted to answer his probing if picked on.

"What's our productivity month to date?" Aubyn asked openly.

The question was not meant for anyone in particular, but he expected an answer.

"26.7 moves per hour, Boss," came a swift reply.

"But it's just day two of the month, still early days yet, Super," added Donovan.

"We all know that by the end of the weekly cycle, when we have completed all the weekly calls, productivity will be back to the 24/25 mark as usual," Steven interjected, with Mark nodding in agreement.

"Perhaps our expectation of decline leads to it," Aubyn suggested.

He had expected their negative feedback, but relished the opportunity to challenge the team's mindset.

"We will achieve 28 moves per hour this month!" Aubyn retorted.

There was a hint of laughter following Aubyn's audacious statement.

"What prevents us from getting there, setting new records, breaking out of the old mold that has us imprisoned? We are gonna do it! We must believe in a vision and work together as a team to get it done. Nothing is impossible!" He continued.

But Aubyn's words, a mixture of probing questions blended with positive affirmations, silenced the laughter and stirred contemplation.

The silence lingered until Garric's voice broke through.

"I believe Super is serious!"

Aubyn recognized the spark in Garric's eyes.

"Are we seriously trying for 28 moves per hour?" Garric's skepticism was apparent and mirrored the collective's thoughts.

"I am sure Aubyn knows how many pieces of equipment are unavailable and how often the available ones break down," Garry thought quietly. "But this is Aubyn we are talking about; he has the information on his smartphone right now, of that, I'm sure."

"There is a hefty incentive payment just waiting to be had, you know," Aubyn said, smiling.

He left them with that thought as he went from the open office area into one of the private offices.

The planning meeting was already in progress, where his core team of operations leaders Chen, William, and Clifton were present. Richard, Mark, and Christopher, three leaders from the maintenance department, were also in attendance.

His next step was to instill this ambitious productivity goal in this core team. Once onboard, they must become purveyors of the new productivity doctrine. In addition, they would indoctrinate critical members of their respective teams, who would then disseminate the vision to their peers.

Key Personal Introspection # 5

Empowering core team members:
·Identify core team members
·Entrust them with the power to influence the vision's outcomes and lead
·Build trust
·Demonstrate how much you value them
·Give room to the dissenting voice
·Provision for conflicting personalities and internal rivalries
·Facilitate role interchange where possible

6

Make it Fun & Inclusive

"Super, I need to chat with you," Kamila called out, halting Aubyn's climb up the stairs to his office.

He was desperate for a quiet moment to process his thoughts. The morning's pace had been relentless. He needed to rehearse the day's events in his mind, step down from his emotional peak to a more analytical calm, and let his rational mind synchronize with his heightened emotions. He needed to ensure he was not overlooking anything that would come back to haunt him or capsize this embryonic wave of energy.

"Sure, walk with me. I'm headed to my office," Aubyn replied.

A discussion with Kamila seldom appealed to logic. These emotionally charged discussions would inevitably end in a spat. Yet, their disagreements were a familiar dance: They argued today to argue again tomorrow. So that was how it was between them. Their conflicts weren't rooted in opposing goals but in their distinct approaches to problem-solving, with neither keen on yielding.

"What shall we name it?" Kamila probed.

"We have to create a brand identity." And with that, Kamila

dove into her self-assumed role as a branding expert or market-ing guru.

"Name what, Kamila? What are you talking about now, Kamila? Brand! what brand?" Aubyn was confused.

"Aubyn, I don't want to argue with you today, but our campaign needs branding. It needs a catchy slogan. I overheard you in the Planning Office. We have to handle this with professionalism. Back in college, I..." Kamila started reminiscing.

"OK, fine, Kamila, do your thing. We'll review what you come up with tomorrow," Aubyn said, interrupting her walk down memory lane.

Possibly, being too drained from the morning's activities to argue, or perhaps he recognized the value in her insights. After all, he couldn't pull this off alone; a collective effort was essential.

And indeed, the project could benefit from being fun and engaging—qualities he wasn't known for. Surely, he would need someone with Kamila's energy and ideas onboard.

"It should have a local flavor so the staff can relate. Make it fun and exciting so the team can resonate with it. Excitement and fun, something the 'operations boss' isn't known for," Kamila joked as she took her leave of him.

"I'll jazz it up a bit, plus I will bring in some creative folks from the department, which will add some spice," she added, departing from his office.

"I said you were in charge, didn't I. You're leading this, remember? Go ahead," Aubyn responded, a trace of a smile on his face.

Finally, Aubyn paused and breathed—a genuine moment of respite amidst the morning's chaos. The ever-present sound of the clanking of metal against metal, the drone of engines, and the warning beeps of gigantic mobile equipment provided the cacophony of sounds. The typical background symphony of a busy terminal.

Sigh!

For what seemed like the first time this morning, Aubyn took a breath.

Leaning back in his chair, he rested one hand on his head, the other tugging at a scrubby, scruffy beard, with eyes closed and his face upturned as if seeking answers from above.

"Actor! Looking pleased with yourself. Got a promotion from Captain B? Or is it the visit from your 'special lady'?" A typical Davidic baseless insinuation, the nature of a rough jest among friends.

"Hey David, good to see you; glad you are here. Your 28 poster inspired me. Recall the Ishikawa Diagram we did seven months back? The one plotting our course to 26 moves per hour? We fell short because we lacked faith, vision, and courage. We missed the boat," Aubyn recounted.

"But now, we will surpass the elusive 28 moves per hour in the next quarter. We have to put on our big boy pants and grow larger cojones," Aubyn retorted enthusiastically.

David slid into the seat across from Aubyn, grasping at the vision his friend had just articulated, easing back and relaxing into the chair as he contemplated.

"Could they evolve to surpass their previous shortcomings, as Aubyn described? Would they step up to meet the challenge? Would the team rally to conquer this herculean task? Aubyn has finally lost it. But count me in. If crazy is what it takes, then I am all in," David pondered silently.

"Alright, we've got some serious work to do; it's time to connect with the grassroots, the everyday people who can make or break this project. We have to hit the ground running. Let's go link up the real people." David was already plotting a plan of action.

"We need to talk to the crane operators; they are the single point of failure. Without their buy-in, we're stuck. I know who to talk to. Let's move! Once again, I'll be having to babysit you. Off to their caravan, we go." Leading the way out, David took charge, with Aubyn on his heels.

So began the energizing of a core group of players, a small group of influencers selected from across all categories of the Operations Team.

Key Personal Introspection # 6

Make it fun and inclusive:
 ·*Lead by inclusion*
 ·*Understand your limitations*
 ·*Seek help from a broad cross-section of persons*
 ·*Recruit persons with strengths you don't possess*
 ·*Make use of team synergies*
 ·*Have an open mind*
 ·*Be willing to learn; you don't know everything*

7

Value People and Their Opinions

"You know, even if we achieve 26 or 27 moves per hour, Captain B may still not confirm you. You might still be just acting," David cautioned.

"To be fair to Captain B, he told me at the time of my initial auditions that Nigel only agreed for me to be appointed on an interim basis," Aubyn reminded David.

The authority had already placed ads internationally to select a long-term operations manager. Aided as they were by the terminal's largest customer.

"But why should that concern us? We have always wanted the opportunity to prove that we locals could do it ourselves. Isn't this what we have always dreamed about? Isn't this what we wanted? Captain B has given me the autonomy to do what I think best," Aubyn continued.

"David, you worry too much. Which team is on duty now? Let's go talk to the guys," Aubyn said, reassuringly placing a hand on his friend's shoulder.

During one of the prior visits to the Operator's Caravan, the idea arose to organize everyone into teams. Initially, only management, supervisors, and office personnel worked four rotating shifts with their respective teams.

The much-maligned rostering system recently implemented assigned the other operations staff members to shifts on a per-needs basis. As far as anyone in the operations knew, this was based on some random, obscure algorithm no one in the department understood.

Aubyn had initially hesitated to embrace this suggested change to having everyone on teams, given his penchant for adhering to technological solutions. Though not directly involved in implementing the rostering system, he recognized its implementation aimed to ensure fair scheduling, eliminate bias or manipulation, and curtail overtime hours.

Six months ago, the overtime hours worked was through the roof. Complaints of schedule manipulation and favoritism arose. Upon investigating, Aubyn realized the new rostering system, like most other tech solutions, wasn't fully understood or optimally employed by the end users.

Lacking the resources to tweak the system, he realized that a team approach would make it much easier for the labor planners to prepare the schedules, given the company's staffing levels and business volume. This was precisely the point the guys in the caravan had made to him that day he had visited.

Aubyn instructed the Labor Planning Team to implement a comprehensive team approach across the operations depart-ment. Clifton aided them in ensuring the balanced composition of each team.

What Aubyn nor the operators clamoring to be placed on teams didn't foresee at the time was the almost immediate impact it would have made: overtime hours dropped by an average of 50% for all labor categories within two months of placing everyone on fixed teams.

Team synergies generated other positive outcomes. The newfound team spirit sparked to life the innate competitiveness among the various groups. These rivalries, which Aubyn helped to stir and, when required, refereed, helped to arrest the decline in productivity. With team spirit at a high, productivity showed signs of fledgling growth.

Many of the tweaks Aubyn had implemented came from similar interactions with various operations team members. Initiatives like 'Done & Go' and the 'Staff Recognition Program for Top Performers' were two such initiatives implemented.

Aubyn duly implemented these suggestions from the staff with no direct cost to the company. In fact, quite the opposite happened. These initiatives were the bedrock and building blocks for achieving the set goals.

It was Friday morning, the third day of the incentive push initiative.

"The Incentive Push Initiative," Aubyn pondered. "Nah, too dull, too drab. Not catchy enough," he muttered aloud.

Before the first of the daily scheduled meetings, in the solitude of his office, he was free to think aloud, whistle a tune, hum a melody, whatever it took to get in the flow. He often lost himself in deep meditative thought, especially early in the morning after dropping off his three little ones at school.

These were the times, away from the responsibilities of home and before his duties at work, that he would use to reconnect to his source. It was a rare time for spiritual reconnection amid the responsibilities of single parenthood, juggling family and work- all of which defined and chiseled and formed the person he had become.

His family, work, and faith completed the circle for him.

However, after his separation, Aubyn took a self-imposed sabbatical from active church duties, finding solace in his kids and job.

These mornings' seclusions afforded him a brief spiritual revival—a chance to be whole again, at least for a moment. His Pastor, Winston, was a tower of strength to him from the first moment they met and never failed to show Aubyn love and support. Even at his lowest point spiritually, Winston was the father, big brother, and friend he needed.

"Maybe someday, he thought to himself, I will be complete again, mind, body, and spirit, but until then, I will pour all of me into all I have."

Aubyn turned his chair toward the window, gazing at the magnificent hills that stretched in every direction. He started reciting a well-known verse.

"I will lift up mine eyes unto the hills, from whence cometh my help. My help cometh from the..."

"LORD! You must be kidding!" Aubyn interrupted his recitation.

The sight of Kamila, with a spring in her steps, heading towards his office disturbed his meditation.

"Thank goodness she's not alone; Doug is with her." Aubyn thought gladly.

Doug was one of the straddle carrier operators Aubyn had bonded with in the rap session David had him do years earlier. By this time, Doug was one of Aubyn's best crane operators, consistently appearing on the top 5 performers list, dubbed "The Kings of the Crane, " thanks to Kamila's unique branding skills.

Doug was the one who suggested re-instituting the staff recognition program for top performers, particularly for crane operators, as the data was readily available, considering there was routine documentation of each crane operator's performance.

"Quick, I could hide under the desk and pretend I'm not here. Or better yet, stand behind the door for five more minutes of peace."

Ahh!" He released a deep, long sigh.

"No, I won't do any such thing, at least not today. I haven't had time to bounce the new Incentive Push Initiative off Doug yet, as he was only returning from his two days off today. Notwithstanding, he always has some relevant and practical ideas." Aubyn said, consoling himself.

"Good morning Super!" they greeted Aubyn in unison.

"Good morning, Kam, Douggie," Aubyn answered in his brightest morning voice.

"Kam, you are up and about early; I thought you would have gotten back to me yesterday. The last time we spoke, you were all fired up. I see you brought some reinforcements with you this morning."

"Dougie, I was expecting you on the afternoon shift. I wanted to touch base with you on a matter, but ..."

"Super! Fantastic idea! I love it!" Doug interjected.

"For a long time now, I've been wondering when we'd address the low productivity for quite some time now. Remember, I told you when you got promoted that most of the guys here have your back? We are on your side. Super, we're ready!" Doug added. Accompanied by the broadest smile on Kamila's face, nodding in agreement.

"Super, CRANK IT UP!" Kamila bellowed with glee.

"Crank it up?" came Aubyn's puzzled reply.

"Yes, CRANK IT UP! That's the slogan. That's what we're all

gonna do. We will crank up the vibes and productivity to levels never seen before," Kamila continued.

"Doug will design some flyers, which we will place all over the terminal. He will create stickers everyone will wear on their safety helmets and clipboards," Kamila said.

The marketing guru was now in her element.

"Leave it to us, Super. We've got this; we have this one locked," Doug assured.

They started for the office door before Kamila spun around, as if she had forgotten something.

"We will need some petty cash, I almost forgot to mention," she said as she parted with a smile.

"Do up a budget, whatever you need," the words seemed to escape from Aubyn without him processing them.

"CRANK IT UP!"

"Yes, crank it up, indeed. I am glad I did not mention my 'Incentive Push Initiative' to them," Aubyn amused himself, laughing out aloud.

"...... LORD, my help cometh from you."

"This was not a terrible start to the morning after all," Aubyn said, continuing his meditation.

Key Personal Introspection # 7

Value people and their opinions:
   ·Leadership equal service
   ·Value those you lead
   ·Listen to persons whom you intend to lead
   ·Value their opinions even if you disagree with it

·*Implement their ideas where possible*
·*Always give credit where credit is due*

8

Lessons From the Past

Doug and Aubyn would have worked on several other projects after that one-hour rap session organized by David.

However, in November 2004, amidst the terminal's operational chaos, the most significant of these projects occurred when a backlog of empty containers stored in the port crippled the terminal's container yard. This was further exacerbated by inadequate leadership at the port.

Mike, a young, brash, ambitious, and outspoken shift manager, openly called out the incompetence of the expats. His outspokenness earned him the task of assembling a team to tackle the problem. One of the same foreign managers he had earlier criticized assigned him the task.

Given his knowledge of the operation and access to the data that drove it, Nathan was the Senior Manager appointed to support the task force. He would provide all the tools and technological expertise the team required to complete the task. Nathan christened the group The Productivity Improvement Task Force (PITK Team). Aubyn and Doug were members of the eight-member team led by Mike that developed, presented, and executed the plan. The PITK Team planned to clear the bottleneck by rearranging over three thousand containers in the main container yard within a 24-hour window.

The PITK team chose Aubyn to present the plan almost by default, as he was the most comfortable speaking about the data emanating from the terminal operating system. He and Mike assumed a lead role as spokespersons when presenting their strategy to Dr. Stark, affectionately known as Doc, and then, with his endorsement, to Nigel 'The Man.'

At that juncture, Doc was Nigel's trusted assistant. Nigel had entrusted Doc with the responsibility of charting the future development of the terminal. Doc led the modernization and development of the port in the late 1990s. He did so in his trademark no-nonsense, combative leadership style. Aubyn was a great admirer of Doc, if not his biggest fan. A Strong personality and effective leadership appealed to Aubyn, so it was no surprise he unreservedly admired Doc.

Aubyn would watch and listen intently each time Doc would visit the IT department to strategize with Nathan.

Just two years prior, Aubyn had felt terrified at the prospect of addressing a group of equipment operators. Now, bolstered by his increased participation in church activities and workplace presentations, he was ready to pitch to two titans of the shipping industry. Deliberately stepping out of his comfort zone had become his habit. He had become accustomed to interacting and mingling with others. This resulted in his growing courage and self-belief.

For more than a year, he had idolized Doc and had a deep understanding of him. Aubyn readily identified with Doc's overall philosophy on port development and operations matters. By the time the presentation came around, he was ready.

It is a popular idiom that people often imitate the ones they admire. So, Doc must have seen a lot of himself in this cocky youngster, as by this time, Aubyn would have unconsciously adopted some of Doc's mannerisms.

The proposal was successful, receiving approval from both Doc and Nigel. Subsequently, the terminal was closed for business for 24 hours to execute the plan. The task force-led endeavor had prepared the terminal for optimal functioning on the resumption of services, restoring the terminal's operational efficiency.

Doc and Nigel did not have a difficult time garnering the consensus of the shipping industry to suspend the terminal's operations for 24 hours, as the terminal was in such dire straits that any meaningful attempts to restore normalcy gained acceptance.

Aubyn had observed that over the years, the terminal goes through these cycles of crisis and fixes. Eight years after the PITK Team was assembled to stem a situation caused partly by poor operation management, here we were again.

The terminal was again in a familiar crisis because of the repeated pattern of operational mismanagement. Coupled with a lack of capital investment, the poor macroeconomic conditions of the country, and the lingering effects of the on-and-off protracted nature of attempts to privatize the terminal.

The major shipping lines patronizing the terminal were becoming increasingly anxious. Their cause for concern was multifaceted.

The terminal's performance was poor, and it continued to head south.

The government was not providing any definitive updates about the timeline for privatizing the terminal. Capital investment in the terminal by the government had all but stalled.

The opening of the new locks of the Panama Canal was imminent. Their stakeholder demanded an answer on how they would position themselves in the region to take advantage of the economies of scale the new lock would afford.

Would they, in fact, could they continue to patronize the terminal, given the level of uncertainty?

Mike, once the audacious shift manager, was now the operations manager. He was to suffer the same fate as all other operations managers before him, regardless of nationality. A failure to learn from past mistakes and successes and mounting external pressures. Mike now faced the operations managers' predicament, as every other manager of recent history had.

As acting operations manager, Aubyn was resolute to break the cycle. He would take control of what he could control.

He revived and applied previous successful strategies, a 'back to basics' approach that yielded more consistent operations performance; this 'back to basics' philosophy helped the operations performances to become less erratic and unpredictable. The operations team's performance was stable, barring acts of God or the far too frequent catastrophic equipment failure, especially the ship-to-shore gantry cranes.

Based on the terminal's designed capacity, vessel traffic, and type of mobile equipment employed, an average productivity of 25 moves per crane hour (MPCH) was attainable. For bigger vessels with more container moves, an average of 27 MPCH was within reach.

Stability in the operations metrics would not cut it, not when the numbers were way below average. Aubyn knew that to surpass the design capacity and achieve upwards of 28 MPCH for a monthly average would require something special. It would take more than just the operations staff. It required an extraordinary collaborative effort, including all the terminal's staff, its customers, and those directly impacted by its activities.

Key Personal Introspection # 8

Learn from the past:
 ·Learn from past failures
 ·Glean from past successes
 ·Do not reinvent the wheel
 ·Innovate and improve on past successes
 ·Where possible, (KISS) Keep It Simple Stupid

9

The Limitless Capacity of the Human Spirit

The Bible mentions God declared that when a united group of people speaking one language set their collective mind on achieving a goal, nothing becomes unattainable. It was early, and Aubyn found himself immersed in deep contemplation.

"This tower stands at a height of just 28 moves per hour, a mere 0.7 higher than the historic peak achieved 61 months ago. The resources were different back then." Aubyn quickly sobered himself and regained his focus.

"Here you go again, fixating on the challenges rather than the possibilities," Aubyn chided himself.

"A good leader comprehends what it means to be under authority. What am I being led by? How well do I follow?" Aubyn pondered.

"I must be led by a higher purpose and have unwavering faith in it. I must commit body, mind, and spirit to follow the desired outcome. It appears my spirit requires a boost," Aubyn smiled to himself.

After two full weeks of CRANK IT UP, all the disciples were

in place, teaching, encouraging, and converting. The converts were many, buoyed by the prospect of earning an incentive, even as The Authority had to impose a wage freeze for the terminal's workforce because of government fiscal constraints.

However, CRANK IT UP's core principles weren't materialistic. Nor were its central precepts based on a doctrine of prosperity or financial rewards. Instead, its core tenets emphasized self-worth, pride, and the joy of accomplishments, with a subtle tint of nationalism.

Aubyn understood CRANK IT UP's success required a narrative transcending mere financial gains. It needed to tap into a deeper, intrinsic motivation to withstand the terminal's shifting dynamics and diminishing resources.

The vagaries of an entity in transition, where nothing was cast in stone, required something more innate to those called to bear its cross at the advent of testing times. This would prove pivotal in the coming months.

With the initial budget for flyers and stickers depleted, Kamila, Doug, and Aubyn out-of-pocketed the additional funds as needed.

The maintenance crews, operations staff, local shipping company staffers, and even contractors proudly wore "CRANK IT UP" on the front and back of their helmets. In contrast, the Office staff, like Kendra, Rossie, and many others who weren't part of the PIS, had stickers on their desks and computers.

Not everyone was fully onboard with adorning themselves with "CRANK IT UP" paraphernalia; some non-believers preferred a wait-and-see approach.

Productivity figures showed marginal improvement at the end of the first month (March), with crane productivity reaching 23.3 MPCH, a modest gain. However, every progress and every victory was celebrated and highlighted. The team put into full effect the local proverb, 'Encouragement sweetens labor.'

By the end of the second month, productivity had averaged an eight-month high of 25.1 MPCH, peaking at an average of 26.2 MPCH in week 16.

Normalcy had returned to crane productivity figures, but instead of resting on their laurels, Aubyn geed up core team leaders to "Crank it up" further. May's productivity averaged above 26 MPCH until a series of significant ship-to-shore crane failures in week 19. But with dogged resolve, the month concluded with a productivity rate of 25.9 MPCH, a one-year high.

June had arrived, the month Aubyn had set as the target to reach the magical 28 MPCH, unlocking the incentive payment. The atmosphere buzzed with excitement, belief, and anticipation, buoyed by three consecutive months of increased productivity.

Every operational activity held significance. Every player understood that their performance contributed to the target's realization.

Even those initially skeptical were now attentive to the KPI Notice Board and were determined to be seen as contributing their fair share and giving their pound of flesh.

Communication channels overflowed with "Crank it up" discussions as each person encouraged and challenged their peers not to falter.

The response time from the Engineers was prompt, if not decisive. The lashers were poetry in motion, briskly maneuvering the twist-locks with newfound vigor. Those lashers who worked from precarious heights were a picture of grace and agility while handling the heavy twist-lock sticks. No one wanted to be fingered as the person who dropped the ball.

"Super, ensure we are part of the Crank It Up celebrations; we are out here cranking it up," one lasher appealed.

"Yes, Super, we are the gears turning your crankshaft," another chimed in.

Although the terminal operators did not directly employ the lashers, they played an integral role in the Operations Team. Some even assumed additional roles as Equipment Operators or Stevedore Coordinators when not performing their stevedore/lashing duties. Aubyn realized that only Arnoldo and Captain B could resolve this issue.

"I'll broach this topic in the next management meeting, plant the seed, and see what germinates from it," Aubyn contemplated.

Key Personal Introspection # 9

Tap into the limitless capacity of the human spirit:
   ·Appeal to the innate abilities of humankind to overcome obstacles
   ·Success begets success
   ·Everyone desires success; show them how to achieve it
   ·People will embrace a vision they perceive will lead to their success
   ·Shared success is sweeter than individual achievements
   ·We have more in common at our core, so speak to that which unites

10

Expect the Unexpected

Aubyn's presentations had evolved into a highly anticipated part of the weekly management meetings. Garnished with graphs and charts prepared for him by his allies, Kendra, who worked out of the finance department, and Alton from the engineering department. He could show how the improved operations performance directly impacted variable costs, the other departments, and overall terminal efficiencies.

His willingness to ask for and receive help and input from those willing to help created the much-needed synergies.

"In week 23, we achieved 28.1 moves per hour, and in week 24, it was an impressive 28.8 moves per hour. As we enter the third week of the month, it's clear to everyone in this room that we are on track to reach the 28 moves per crane hour target," Aubyn exclaimed, beaming with immense pride in his team's accomplishments.

However, the real reason for emphasizing the impending milestone stemmed from the previous day's conversation with the lashers.

Aubyn continued, "I recognize we discontinued the Lashers'

Incentive Scheme years ago. However, the current status quo has them intricately interwoven into the fabric of our operations. It is inconceivable to consider paying an incentive without their inclusion."

This ignited a lively debate, ultimately leading to a consensus in favor of including the lashers; neglecting them would be counterproductive.

When it was Arnoldo's turn to present, he carefully outlined the company's financial position, the below-budgeted volumes, and the disproportionately high fixed cost structure.

"Our elevated fixed costs offset the savings from the reduction in variable cost gained by increased productivity. Therefore, our best chance to achieve financial resilience is to maintain strong operational performance that will attract additional business," he posited. Hence, without the additional volumes, the terminal is not in a position to take on any additional costs.

"We still have the PIS obligation to honor," Aubyn interjected.

"And we will uphold our commitment, as long as it remains, and if all the numbers compute for a payout, in keeping with established international benchmarks," Arnoldo rebutted.

The phrase in Arnoldo's statement, 'in keeping with international benchmarks,' struck Aubyn.

"We have two KPIs to meet for a payout," Aubyn confidently stated, backed by information from Nathan.

"Crane Productivity above 28 moves per hour and Crane Reliability exceeding 98.1% are the only requirements. Both KPIs are being met," Aubyn noted, directing his gaze at Uncle Glen, the maintenance manager.

"We know we haven't reached the Straddle Carrier Availability target yet, but the weight of the other indicators is sufficient," he added.

"Well, The Authority has expressed some legitimate concerns about the measurement of the Crane Reliability KPI, so let's see where the numbers stand at the end of the month. Until then, keep up the excellent work," and with that said, Arnoldo concluded his presentation.

Aubyn recognized that there was one person who could provide authoritative insights into the Crane Reliability KPI.

"Hey, Professor, what's the story with the maintenance KPIs, specifically Crane Reliability?"

Aubyn contacted Nathan right after the meeting.

Truth be told, Aubyn and the other senior operations managers had always been skeptical of how the maintenance department calculated their KPI metrics. Even during challenging times, their reported reliability figures did not seem to align with the actual situation on the ground. Maintenance KPIs were not as cut and dry as Operational KPIs.

Nathan clarified that the Authority had adopted the international industry standard for measuring the said KPI, as the existing method did not align with best practices. He explained that he had updated all the relevant dashboards and reports to reflect this standard.

Given the ongoing challenges in the maintenance department, it was unlikely that they would meet this KPI anytime soon; of that, Aubyn was certain.

Aubyn inquired, "What does this mean for the incentive?"

"Well, the team would need to achieve an average of 29 moves per hour for the month," Nathan responded reassuringly, if not optimistically.

Aubyn didn't doubt his team's ability to meet this new target. They had reached a weekly average of 28.8 MPCH the previous week, with plenty of room for improvement.

However, this change to the goalpost, just as most of the team was believing and hoping for better things to come, raised questions.

How would they react to this new information? Would they trust Aubyn's words after this? Was he about to face his worst fear of losing the trust of his team? The trust he had painstakingly built was at risk of being lost.

Key Personal Introspection # 10

Expect the unexpected:
·*Remain vigilant*
·*There will be bumps in the road*
·*Remain calm and keep the faith*
·*Keep your eyes fixed on the prize and keep moving forward*
·*When there is a significant purpose in what you do when faced with adversity, double down and keep pushing*
·*Be agile and willing to adjust quickly*

11

Be Honest

Aubyn realized he needed a moment to compose his thoughts. For the first time since the onset of the Crank It Up initiative, the feeling of being swamped had caught him off guard, and he felt overwhelmed.

It should have been clear to him. How could he have overlooked such a maneuver or missed that trick?

" I allowed myself to get caught up in the moment's excitement and failed to see this coming," he chided himself silently.

"The only way forward is to be upfront about this new twist with my team. I will level with the team by providing a full update on this latest development. I must try to get in front of this before the team hears rumors and misinformation from other sources."

Leaning back, eyes shut, Aubyn took a moment to steady his nerves.

He understood the urgency of controlling the narrative. Rumors would spread quickly. There would be those seeking to discredit the entire Crank It Up effort as another management hoax, a ruse to extract more work from employees with no tangible reward. Another deception to make the workers labor slavishly for a reward that would never come.

He was already under subtle pressure to keep the team's performance just shy of triggering the incentive payout.

"People expect you to see the larger picture now, Aubyn. You're a senior manager," they said.

"Look at things from the company's perspective. Keep productivity just under the incentive threshold. It's a win-win. There's a promise of a bonus in December for hitting near the 26/27 moves per hour target while keeping our customers content."

But he obstinately pushed forward with the Crank It Up campaign. He resisted all attempts of persuasion or reasoning not aligned with the mission of maximizing the worker's potential. Also, given the entity's budgetary constraints, he should have known that some other method would have been found to avoid a significant financial payout.

But they didn't grasp that Aubyn's commitment wasn't to the incentives. Aubyn had always believed the terminal was not performing to its potential. The desire to see the terminal's workforce fulfill their potential helped fuel his passion.

He became even more resolute in that belief over the last month. Although they were achieving record-high productivity, there was still much room for improvement toward achieving greater efficiency.

He would argue that the actual big picture is beyond just the incentive.

"A productivity incentive scheme is a means, not the end. An incentive payment is not the goal; maximum efficiency is," Aubyn argued.

Revitalized after refreshing his spirit for a moment, Aubyn dismissed his skepticism, set aside his doubts, and repented of his unbelief.

He then embarked on one of his impassioned crusades throughout the terminal, eager to share the new revelation with the team. Using the change in the crane reliability KPI as a source of motivation. His new refrain was, "When the going gets tough, the tough gets going."

The first round of interactions restored his confidence. As usual, he would benefit significantly from the exchanges. His willingness to share himself honestly with others. To be vulnerable by discussing his fears, hopes, and expectations. As he tried to lift others' spirits, it proved not only to be cathartic, but the positive feedback from the team and the commitment to the cause, both in words and deeds, lifted him to new heights.

Chen, his planning manager, was a very pragmatic guy and a whiz at Microsoft Excel, which he used with aplomb to strategize effectively for the upcoming weeks.

"Super, these are the vessels we have for the rest of the month. We must hit these targets on each call to achieve 29 moves per hour and above." Chen outlined.

And so it was, with most of the people Aubyn met. They were just as committed. They understood the stakes and knew what the situation demanded of them.

It was already halfway through the month, and reaching 29 MPCH by month's end seemed increasingly daunting. It was week 25, and the figures had dipped below the previous week's high of 28.8 MPCH.

Based on the recent history of two service calls, Chen had alerted the team of two particularly challenging ships expected the following week. The terminal's performance on these ships would be crucial to hitting the target.

"We'll need to average a minimum of 30 moves per hour in

these last two weeks to reach 29 moves per hour," Chen had advised.

Week 25 closed with productivity of 27.5 MPCH, down 4.5% from the week before, with no significant equipment breakdowns to blame. There could be only one reason for the decline in productivity: a reaction to the changes in the KPI calculations voiced during that week.

The Core Team members did all they could to control the narrative. They put a positive spin on the ensuing discussions, which were inevitable with such a change in the KPI computations. The timing of these changes was the most contentious issue being contended.

Aubyn and his core team of managers would scan the radio channels, shoring up belief and ensuring the narrative was optimistic and upbeat. As a result, the team kept morale high and the outlook positive through all communication channels.

The spirit of determination and the sense of purpose within the core team were palpable. By mid-week 26, Chen's projections showed they needed to sustain an average of 32 MPCH to meet the new 29 MPCH goal confidently. It was all or nothing for that week.

Aubyn's phone buzzed.

"Super!" It was Chen.

"About the problematic ships we discussed?"

"Yeh Chen, the first one's ETA is tomorrow night. Are we set for a stellar performance on it this weekend?" Aubyn asked.

"No need Super! It's been delayed because of engine trouble and will not arrive until next week. As for the other problematic one, it won't be loading. The agent just advised that it is unloading all its cargo, then going to anchorage, a total discharge only," Chen updated him.

In the operations, the unloading/discharge process is usually faster than the loading, and the productivity is even better for vessels unloading all the containers.

Hanging up, Aubyn couldn't help but feel a sense of destiny.

"If I wasn't a believer before, I certainly am now. The universe really seems to align for those who have faith and act on it," he reflected.

However, while destiny bellowed beyond the weekend's horizon, Aubyn felt the pangs of conflict gnawing away at the pit of his stomach: work or family. Which would it be?

Key Personal Introspection # 11

Be honest:
   ·To win and maintain trust, one has to be honest
   ·Be open and share your inner thoughts
   ·You need not be pretentious; others can identify with your vulnerabilities
   ·Be positive and share those positive energies
   Be inspired by the good you see in others

12

The Sweet Taste of Victory

Aubyn faced a pressing dilemma on this most important of weekends: choosing between a family reunion with relatives arriving from abroad and being in the trenches with the team for this crucial project phase. To help him find a compromise, Aubyn consulted his friend and mentor for advice on how he could attend his family reunion while keeping a finger on the terminal's pulse.

Nathan's cell was ringing; it was Aubyn again. They had been in constant communication over the past week. Nathan acted as a solution provider and a source of encouragement for his young friend. Nathan may not have known it, but his endless optimism and words of encouragement were a beacon for Aubyn during this time.

"Hey Nathan, I'm in a bind," Aubyn shared, his voice tinged with perplexity.

Nathan attentively heard out the complexities troubling Aubyn.

"Aubyn, prioritize your family. I'll set up the productivity monitors to update you every hour. We've been fine-tuning a web-based productivity dashboard. I'll send you the link to access it throughout the weekend."

With Nathan's assurance, Aubyn felt a newfound calm about his weekend plans.

"Why was I so stressed?" Aubyn pondered.

"The groundwork has been laid. It's now up to each team member's dedication to hit our targets. I believe in our staff's commitment and ability to rise to the challenge."

True to his word, Nathan ensured Aubyn received hourly productivity reports.

The veracity of the productivity updates depended on how prompt Clayton and Denton keyed in the completed vessels in the system, both of whom pledged to log overtime that weekend to ensure the timeliest updates possible.

Throughout the weekend, the incoming reports thrilled Aubyn. The team was working at a record pace, well on track to surpass the 32 MPCH Chen had projected to achieve the recomputed monthly target of 29 MPCH.

The stats were impressive:
  ·Beijing: 1054 moves @ 31.1 MPCH
  ·Ritscher: 291 moves @ 35.9 MPCH
  ·Qingdao: 1407 moves @ 40.8 MPCH
  ·Colombo: 494 moves @ 48.0 MPCH
  ·San Antonio: 679 moves @ 30.6 MPCH
  ·Ela: 450 moves @ 30.8 MPCH
  ·Rostock: 434 moves @ 36.8 MPCH

As the month concluded, the team's productivity was at an all-time high, working toward a collective goal.

On Monday, July 1st, Aubyn entered the terminal's parking lot with a sense that something positive had shifted. Leading up to this moment, the mood of the workers was lively and optimistic. A growing sense of anticipation occurs when one is on the verge of achieving some monumental feat.

But what Aubyn was sensing today was more than optimism, more than the belief that says, 'I CAN.' Instead, there was a knowing, a living in the present moment that says, 'I AM.' A winning 'I AM' mentality that, once held in conscious awareness, knows no defeat.

Everyone moved with a spring in their step; everyone seemed taller, and even David looked to have gained much-needed height.

"We did it, Aubyn! We exceeded even our greatest expectations," David shouted from across the parking lot as he rushed over to greet Aubyn, extinguishing a cigarette as he made his way over.

"Anything is possible, of this I am sure, even you look 5 feet 7 inches today," Aubyn responded, beaming from ear to ear.

"Maybe now you can stop putting that poison into your body," Aubyn continued.

"Don't mek mi start on your case today; let's enjoy the victory; later, I will deal with you," came the quick response from David.

Aubyn met Clayton and Denton later that morning. He implored them to ensure that they double-checked the veracity of the reported statistics and looked out for any discrepancy or padding of the numbers from the execution team. They assured him they had audited all the numbers and corrected any discrepancies.

"Don't worry yourself, Super. We have everything under control and in order," Clayton assured him.

"Just remember that there will be an audit from the quality

assurance and the finance teams before any incentive is paid." Aubyn reminded them.

After finalizing all the vessels, the system computation for last week's productivity was 32.9 MPCH. After the initial audit check and some minor adjustments, June's official weighted average crane productivity was 29.2 MPCH—enough for incentive payouts and a record performance for the terminal, surpassing the previous high of 27.3 MPCH from February 2009. Before the audit check and minor adjustments that would come about later, June's productivity stood at 29.4 MPCH.

The team had completed the proverbial tower of Babel; now, there is a need to ensure that the prevailing narrative continues to facilitate understanding and unity of purpose, coupled with the 'I AM' mentality. There would be no time or place for complacency.

Key Personal Introspection # 12

In victory, remain focused:
·*Enjoy your victories*
·*Learn all you can from it*
·*Remain focused on your purpose*
·*One victory may not end the war or future wars*
·*Winning is a state of mind or consciousness*
·*A winning mentality is the ultimate prize*
·*Victory follows At–One–Ment, Peace of mind and enlightenment*

13

Celebration Time

A strong team spirit, hard work and dedication had triggered the incentive. The month's production totaled 72,760 moves, representing an adverse variance of some 17,694 container vessel moves compared to the budgeted volume of 90,454 vessel moves.

The maintenance performance metrics stabilized, though remaining notably below the set goals. However, a surge in productivity across all departments brought about additional benefits.

- Hourly Gang production increased by 7.4%
- Electric consumption per crane move decreased by an average of 18.8% since initiating the Crank It Up initiative
- Fuel consumption for each container handled was also moving towards the target
- A net weighted crane productivity of 29.2 MPCH represented a 12.7% improvement from May's 25.9 MPCH

Despite these gains, the disproportionately high Fixed Costs due to lower-than-expected container volumes impacted the finances. Shipping lines, driven by economic factors, determine a port's container throughput. While terminal efficiency is a factor, container throughput on a transshipment terminal is a lagging indicator in response to shipping line strategies, which are intricately linked to the sustainability of the lines and the terminals they patronize.

The port required an upsurge in volumes and additional capital investments, neither of which was imminent. Yet, the entity would fulfill its commitment to the active incentive scheme within a fortnight.

Much credit must be given to Nigel, the president of The Authority; Captain B and Arnoldo from the terminal's management; Adrian, the chief union delegate; and Mr. Henry Haase, the General Secretary of the trade union, who honored this commitment.

They didn't just meet the agreement terms; they went above and beyond. Recipients under the PIS scheme received their due reward, and the lashers were similarly compensated. There was a celebration to commemorate the historic achievement, which coincided with the incentive payout. Kamila, who had the ear of Captain B, played a significant role in organizing the Crank It Up Celebrations.

The festivities extended beyond the terminal staff. Distinguished guests and other VIPs from the wider shipping industry attended the main event, where Nigel, Captain B, and Aubyn delivered speeches. Mr. Henry Haase was not to be outdone; adorned in the finest attire, he gave a most memorable address to his constituents.

A variety of performances showcased the workforce's diverse talents. Aubyn's highlight was Ms. Flo-Ann Campbell's "Crank

It Up" Dub poetry, which encapsulated the campaign's spirit and hinted at a future of limitless promise.

Aubyn was now reclining at his desk, basking in his team's success and reflecting on how the management of the Terminal and The Authority had fulfilled their promise to the staff by paying all operational staff the earned incentive. The staging of last week's grand celebration event also exceeded their obligatory responsibility.

Little did he realize that the buzzing of the office phone was an ominous signal of a viperous sting in the tail.

Key Personal Introspection # 13

Celebrate milestones:
- *Honor commitments made*
- *Reward excellence*
- *Give on to Caesar what is due unto Caesar*
- *Recognize a person's contribution*
- *Delight in the successes of others*
- *Be inclusive even in victory*
- *While celebrating, don't lose sight of the big picture*

14

Fact or Fiction

It was 1700 hours, and Aubyn was preparing to sign out for the day. His thoughts wandered to the previous week's events, but the ringing of his phone interrupted the moment. The number on the display belonged to the Board Room.

"Hello, Aubyn. Please join us in the Board Room," said Liam, the HR Manager, on the other end of the line.

It was unusual for Liam to request a meeting at this hour, but Aubyn thought little of it.

"This shouldn't take long. I'll still be on time to pick up the kids after their activities," he mused. Aubyn prided himself on being present for his children, often arriving early to watch and help with their extracurriculars.

The Board Room was the same conference room used for weekly management meetings, with space to seat sixteen. When Aubyn entered, the meeting was already in progress. He quietly slipped into one of the vacant seats. Captain B sat at the head of the table, with Arnoldo, Liam, Samuel, and Faith (the Internal Auditor) strategically positioned opposite the empty chairs.

An eerie silence greeted him as Aubyn entered, and a hush fell over the proceedings. Captain B acknowledged his arrival and immediately explained the purpose of the meeting.

"Faith and Samuel's audit team uncovered significant fraudulent activities in the reporting of operational metrics," he began, his voice heavy with measured authority. "This is unlike anything I've witnessed in all my years on the port."

Captain B explained that the alleged fraud had resulted in considerable financial costs. Because of the gravity of the situation, he said, contacting the police fraud squad is typically required.

"I knew of this before last week's celebrations," he admitted. "But I felt it was only fair to proceed with the event. Most of the staff had no involvement in this and deserved recognition for their efforts toward increased productivity, despite any embellishments in the final computations."

Aubyn sat motionless in total silence, thoughts ambling in and out of his mind. It was as if he were experiencing an out-of-body trance, observing the scene from a distance. His thoughts wandered to similar moments in his life—near-misses on the road, his first time speaking publicly at church—moments where time slowed, and he was both a participant and an observer.

In this meta-cognitive state of awareness, Aubyn resolved to hold his peace, dispassionately absorbing the unfolding drama. Samuel and Faith outlined their findings, explaining that the Shift Managers' end-of-shift reports falsely claimed high-wind delays to crane operations, discrepancies revealed by data from the crane's PLC database, among other findings.

Aubyn listened keenly and took mental notes as he did.

"Many of the report's findings were based on limited knowledge of the operations and other inaccurate assumptions. However, refuting a subjective analysis with counterarguments may not be enough," Aubyn pondered.

Arnoldo spoke next, his voice laden with disappointment.

"Aubyn, I can't express how let down I feel," Arnoldo said, his tone sharp. "You've always been a brilliant, promising lad. But to orchestrate something like this? It's unacceptable."

Arnoldo leaned forward, his words cutting deeper. "Operations Managers before you—some with years of international experience—couldn't achieve those KPIs. But somehow, we're expected to believe you did? Faced with the Terminal's current challenges! What makes you so special?"

Aubyn felt a spark of emotion for the first time—a pang of wounded pride. His ego grabbed at the controls of his once placid demeanor. Now, as a full-time participant in the unfolding drama, the calm detachment he'd maintained crumbled as he wrestled with his demons manfully. His awareness of the observer had all but vanished.

Liam spoke next, his tone gentler but firm. "Aubyn, you must respond to the audit report within the next twenty-four hours." He handed over the report. "Review it and consider your response carefully."

Captain B concluded the meeting, his voice steady but somber. "It's fortunate the Terminal's internal auditors discovered this. If the Authority had uncovered it, the consequences would be far more severe—it could have escalated to a criminal investigation."

"The meeting, brief but heavy, ended within fifteen minutes. At least I got that one thing right," Aubyn murmured dumbfoundedly as he left the room, his thoughts a whirlwind of uncertainty.

And with that, the meeting concluded, leaving Aubyn to

contemplate his next move.

Key Personal Introspection # 14

Faced with great adversity:

- Maintain your composure
- *Listen more: Speak less*
- *Be the observer*
- Be aware of your thoughts/emotions
- *Do not judge your accusers*
- Do not judge yourself
- *Be dispassionate*

15

Lean On Me

When Aubyn left the terminal that evening, his emotions churned in a chaotic mix. The soaring confidence he had felt last week, when everything seemed to align perfectly, now felt like a distant memory. Anger, betrayal, unworthiness, righteous indignation, and a prevailing sense of being overwhelmed all wrestled for dominance in his mind. Unsure of which emotion to cling to, he did the only thing that made sense—he sought the persons closest to him for support—those who held his hands throughout this journey.

"Hello, Nathan. I need your help with something," Aubyn said, his voice heavy with exhaustion and despair.

Nathan listened intently as Aubyn recounted the meeting's events and the audit's conclusions. His response was calm and deliberate, almost as though he had expected this moment. Nathan's voice was as peaceful and reassuring as Aubyn's was despondent.

"Aubyn, remember that the dashboard metrics compute in real time and are not influenced by the Shift Managers' End of Shift Reports. The manual reports match the dashboard results closely. I suggest you remove all the delays attributed to high winds. You'll see the impact on the final computation is negligible," Nathan reassured him.

"Get some rest, Aubyn, and tackle the audit report tomorrow. You've got this!" With those comforting words, Nathan bade him good night.

Next on his call list was David. Aubyn hesitated, knowing what kind of fiery response he could expect. He wanted a more precise plan before facing David's energy, and he did not want to call Kendra until he was home and had some solitude. After mentally preparing himself, he ultimately dialed David's number. Aubyn considered using Nathan's reassurance to assure his friend David that everything would be alright.

"Yow, David, you wouldn't believe what just happened," Aubyn began.

As expected, David reacted with pure indignation. As Aubyn explained the meeting events to him, he became increasingly belligerent.

"Aubyn, only you they'd try this BS with. I would've rained hellfire down on their heads! Where were they when we were working night and day to hit this target? They didn't believe in us, and now this!" David was seething. "That's why they had you acting in the position for so long and haven't appointed you, even after all you had done to stabilize the ship. They are probably still actively seeking to replace you with another expat."

David was livid, but his words mirrored Aubyn's thoughts, especially immediately after Arnoldo spoke during the meeting—words of anger that his persona would not allow him to express openly.

Aubyn tried to temper David's frustration. "That's true, David.

I felt the same. But Nathan said the numbers will still exceed 29 MPCH if we remove the wind delays. So no burning down of Babylon just yet. Plus, the other stuff in the report can be easily refuted. The audit team clearly doesn't understand how the operations department functions or what events are legitimate delays."

David's voice remained defiant. "You can play nice. First thing tomorrow, I'll be in your office and I'll draft the response to that bogus audit report for you to send."

Finally, after getting his kids settled in for the night, Aubyn reached out to Kendra.

"Hey, Aubyn," Kendra greeted warmly. "I got wind of the audit report yesterday but couldn't give you a heads-up and compromise myself. But I know the work you and the team put in to ensure those reports are accurate. That'll stand you in good stead."

Their conversation stretched over an hour, with Kendra's calming presence helping to ease Aubyn's tension. By the end, he confessed, "I can't sleep without responding to this tonight. But after talking to you, David, and Nathan, I feel ready to face it. I am in a much better place mentally."

By 2130 hours, Aubyn was back in his office, methodically addressing each point in the audit report. He clarified misconceptions, corrected false assumptions, and refuted baseless conclusions. The only task left was recomputing June's MPCH without the high-wind delays. For that, he needed his Revenue Assurance team. He emailed Denton and Clayton, outlining the task and requesting them to update the figures first thing in the morning. Before logging out, he sent his initial response to the audit team, committing to provide the revised MPCH by the end of the next business day. With the weight lifted, he headed home, determined to get a good night's rest.

The following morning, Clayton called. "Hey, Super. We completed the task and updated the system with the new figures." Denton's voice echoed in the background, affirming their work.

Aubyn's heart raced. "And the new number?"

Clayton replied confidently, "Before the change, 29.4 MPCH. After removing the wind delays, it's 29.2 MPCH."

Denton chimed in, "Super, we're still good. Nothing to worry about. Why did you ever doubt?"

Aubyn chuckled in relief. "From now on, no more high-wind delays unless the cranes actually shut down because of wind." He paused. "I will get that message out to the team. You and Clayton have done a fantastic job in ensuring the Shift reports are accurate, and I am really proud of how quickly you both recomputed the metrics."

Three months and several audits later, the audit team declared its satisfaction with the integrity of the Shift Reports. June's incentive payment was the first of several similar payments that would follow in the proceeding months for sustained levels of high productivity. Even when financial constraints forced the curtailment of incentive payments, productivity improvement continued its relentless march. When Aubyn transitioned leadership to William in March 2014, the Operations Team carried on his legacy, setting new records and redefining performance benchmarks.

Aubyn's perseverance and the unwavering support of his team and the many other believers, both on and off the terminal, created the momentum that laid a foundation for lasting success: Harnessing the synergies of team belief.

Key Personal Introspection # 15

Learn to lean on others when necessary:

- *No man is an Island*
- Cultivate a strong support system
- *Lean on your support system as needed*
- *Be self-aware*
- Pursue a robust mental health
- *Meditate*
- *Cultivate mindfulness*

16

Final Reflections

For Aubyn, this Crank It Up journey held immeasurable signif-icance. Although he can recount the start of the crank-it-up mission on the port, he knows well that his personal journey of self-improvement reflected the infinite potential of human consciousness. Just as consciousness has no clear beginning or end, Aubyn knew that his journey of self-improvement would be a lifelong pursuit that would require dedication, discipline, and unwavering commitment. Most of all, such a journey requires a never-ending sequence of conscious decisions to achieve some set goal.

So, in 2013, he found himself at a crossroads, a moment in time. Instead of recoiling from it, he embraced the opportunity.

Aubyn made the purposeful decision and dove in wholeheart-edly, mind, body, and spirit, unlike three years prior, when he was the control tower manager and did not fully commit to the moment. He cast aside his fears and misgivings, altogether reconciling himself to the HERE and NOW, willing to accept all it presented.

In this moment of enlightenment, he realized that the aloofness in which he had once sought refuge no longer served him.

He realized that each moment teemed with the potential for deep personal connections. He gave himself over to these opportunities, and hence, many of the bonds forged during his quarter-century-long sojourn on the port continue to flourish today. Many people he encountered along the way significantly impacted his life's journey.

Not least amongst them is the lifelong union he shares with Kendra, his onetime ally from the finance department. Kendra was a relative newbie to the port. She came on board a few months before Captain B appointed Aubyn as acting operations manager. She quickly became a shining star in the finance department because of her foresight and keen analytical mind. This made her a treasured asset to both Arnoldo and Captain B. And her opinions may have mattered beyond financial issues.

Aubyn and Kendra first met at a meeting Arnoldo convened with the operations management team. Arnoldo invited David and Aubyn, who then worked in the business solutions department.

Kendra's financial analysis revealed that the operations team was hemorrhaging as a cost center. Hence, Arnoldo's invitation to David and Aubyn counterbalanced those of the operations managers.

Maybe the combative brashness of Aubyn "ala his icon Doc" and his knowledge of the operations and its terminal operating system impressed Kendra and appealed to her analytical mind. She would later suggest to Arnoldo and Captain B to give the young imposter, Aubyn, the opportunity to put his cards on the table and show his worth as operations manager.

Nigel had requested a change in the operation's leadership, bowing to the mounting pressure from the wider local and international shipping community.

Aubyn was unaware of Kendra's endorsement. However, he should have taken the hint, as his ally in the finance department helped ensure his success in the acting role with her weekly analytical graphs, which were vital to his understanding of the impact of operational activities on the entity's financial status.

Nigel and the leadership of the terminal's largest customers sanctioned the decision to appoint Aubyn. The appointment to that critical position required consensus.

A consensus that was pivotal in the team's achievement, the success of which depended on the cooperation and support of operatives from across the industry.

T-Mac and Franco were two of Aubyn's former managers when he first came to the port and worked at the CFS (Container Freight Station), and they both significantly impacted him. Upon T-Mac's promotion to a senior operations management role, he boasted about an outstanding young lad at the CFS (Aubyn) who should be earmarked for a future leadership role. When a Vessel Planner position became available—a position much sought after by most young operations team members, as it was a significant step on the rung upward—Franco, Aubyn's CFS manager, encouraged him to seize the opportunity. Aubyn was unaware of the significance of this opportunity, as he knew little about the company's inner workings besides the CFS operations. However, with Franco's mentorship, he accepted the promotion to the position of Vessel Planner. As fate would have it, when Aubyn accepted the promotion to Assistant Operations Manager (Yard), he was sandwiched between T-Mac and Franco, two of the four Assistant Managers. Aubyn would serve as the shift relief for T-Mac, and Franco would relieve him at the end of his shift. Once again, these two senior operations leaders took Aubyn under their wings and molded him for the success he enjoyed in this new role. T-Mac and Franco had distinct personalities, but Aubyn took golden nuggets from both men.

Gabby was another person who had a lasting impact on Aubyn. He was once the head of operations when Aubyn was the control tower manager, and their operational philosophy clashed several times during Gabby's tenure.

However, Gabby never failed to allow Aubyn the freedom to express himself openly without fear of reprisal or disapproval. Through his example, Gabby taught Aubyn effective management of strong and opinionated people, even when their opinions differed.

Another of these bonds was with Doc, who would later take on the role of mentor to Aubyn after Godfrey, the new head of The Authority, appointed Aubyn to succeed Captain B.

Aubyn, a longtime admirer of Doc, would benefit immensely from their close working relationship during this time. Both Doc and Godfrey helped Aubyn shepherd the terminal through the rocky path, which was privatization.

Godfrey became a friend and mentor to Aubyn, entrusting him with the responsibility of leading the terminal. Aubyn became the youngest person in the terminal's history to be appointed in that role. Godfrey ensured he had all the support he needed to navigate the terminal's transitional period. In Godfrey, Aubyn found a confidante, someone he trusted and who trusted him.

Then there was Erwan Sr, the CEO of the newly privatized terminal, who appointed Aubyn as his deputy. Erwan mentored Aubyn and exposed him to different management philosophies, specifically those of a large multinational port operator. To Erwan's credit, he maintained the Crank It Up spirit for the duration of his tenure. Hence, the terminal consistently ranked in the top position for the shipping conglomerate.

Along his journey, Aubyn learned to recognize the reflection of his own essence in his peers and those he led, those who referred to him as Boss or Super. There was a profound unity in their shared mission, a sense of oneness that transcended mere camaraderie.

He also saw different aspects of himself in those he respected and emulated, icons like Pastor Winston, Doc, Nathan, Gabby, Godfrey, and Erwan Snr. He understood that the traits he admired in them were not just aspirational, but were already present within the nucleus of his being.

On a spiritual level, his notion of a deity was interwoven within the fabric of his existence; nothing could separate him from the divine essence that animated his life. In it, he lived, moved, and had his being.

He found that this revelation about himself was universal, a truth applicable to all humanity. In this unity, he found completion and reclaimed a sense of wholeness and interconnectedness through this collective "Crank It Up" endeavor.

Each individual was distinct, yet part of a more significant, inseparable whole—unique in their contributions but one in purpose and existence.

"Long may this journey continue! Keep on cranking it up for life!" declared Aubyn.

Glossary of Terms

Productivity: The average move per crane hour for all gantry cranes.

Moves per crane hour (MPCH): The average number of container lifts per crane hour for all STS gantry cranes.

Ship-to-Shore Gantry Crane (STS): A large gantry crane in a container terminal/port that loads and unloads containers from vessels.

Key Performance Indicators (KPIs): Measurable and quantifiable metrics used to evaluate the performance of the terminal's operational activities against set targets.

Equipment (Crane) Reliability: The percentage of time the cranes perform reliably in moving containers to and from the ship during vessel operations.

Equipment (Straddle Carrier) Availability: The percentage of straddle carriers available for the operations at the start of each shift.

Terminal Operating System (TOS): A management software designed for container terminals to control the port's movement and storage of containers (and other cargo). The systems optimize the use of labor and equipment, plan workload, and facilitate the flow of electronic data interchange (up-to-date information) in real-time.

Productivity Incentive Scheme (PIS): A productivity bonus scheme to incentivize all shift workers to increase vessel productivity. The Productivity Incentive Scheme (PIS) was based on the following performance indicators:

·Productivity: >= 28 MPCH

·Crane Reliability (%): >= 98.1

·Straddle Carrier Availability (%): >= 89.0

Lasher: A person who performs general stevedoring duties, mainly but not limited to container and cargo lashing, unlashing, and affixing twist-locks to secure the containers.

Twist-locks: A locking mechanism used to secure shipping containers together during transport. Container twist locks work by fastening the twist lock device into each of the four corner posts.

PLC: A programmable logic controller (PLC) is an industrial computer adapted for controlling machine activities that require high reliability, ease of programming, and process fault diagnosis.

CFS: A Container Freight Station (CFS) is a warehouse that consolidates and de-consolidates cargo for shipping. It is located near ports, airports, and railway hubs.

About the Author

I am a retired shipping executive with over 25 years of experience at a major container terminal in the Americas. I take pride in having been part of a team that achieved record-breaking productivity during a challenging economic period. Despite the obstacles, we remained focused on our goals and worked tirelessly to ensure the terminal operated at peak efficiency. As a tribute to our success, I have written this memoir commemorating our achievement, which serves as a reminder that with worker buy-in and significant team synergies, anything is possible.

www.ingramcontent.com/pod-product-compliance
Lightning Source LLC
Chambersburg PA
CBHW071359130726
47996CB00002B/995